Contents

CW01084904

Introduction

No one knows for certain exactly how many trade union workplace representatives there currently are, but estimates put the number anywhere between 200,000 and 400,000.

According to the influential 1992 report *Workplace Industrial Relations in Transition* (WIRS), which analysed the state of workplace industrial relations, including trade union representation, the average workplace representative is responsible for somewhere between 20 and 30 workers, depending on the size of the workplace.

The report describes workplace representatives as "one of the most visible indicators of trade union organisation on the ground and an important adjunct of recognition".

Trade union workplace representatives are therefore vital to trade union influence in the workplace. Most, although not necessarily all, workplaces where unions are recognised have appointed workplace representatives. Their job is, as a minimum, to act:

- as a primary channel of communication between local members and management; and
- as the basic building block upon which more complex forms of union organisation can be established.

As this booklet will explain, the role and status of the union workplace representative has been challenged by a change to the law which takes away from union representatives their exclusive rights to be consulted over certain workplace-related issues. The booklet looks at how union representatives can best defend members' interests and those of the workforce overall in these changed circumstances.

The TUC has been consulting its affiliated member unions on the role of workplace representatives and its publication, *Your Voice at Work*, adopted by the 1995 TUC Congress, offers detailed proposals for a change in the law, aimed at strengthening union rights and guaranteeing proper representation at work.

The decline in union membership since 1979 has had an impact on the overall number of representatives in workplaces. According to the WIRS report, workplaces with low levels of union membership are now more likely not to have representatives. The table below shows the proportion of workplaces with union representatives and also whether they have just one representative or more than one.

Table 1: Union representatives in the workplace

	At least one rep	Senior rep	Full time rep
All industries	38%	12%	1%
Where the union is recognised	71%	22%	2%

Source: *Workplace Industrial Relations in Transition*

Union recognition is clearly of major importance in gaining a workplace representative, although more than a quarter of workplaces where recognition has been conceded still do not have a representative. Senior representatives (often known as "convenors") are relatively rare, while the proportion of workplaces with representatives on 100% facility time is fairly low.

One of the reasons why workplaces with recognition remain without rep-

" ARMED WITH THE FACTS "

resentatives may be because union members are unwilling to come forward to do what they perceive to be a difficult task which could even put their job prospects in jeopardy. That is why a booklet like this is so essential: for new reps; those contemplating standing as representatives; and, of course, for those who have been in the job for a while, but nevertheless feel it is important to keep up to date with legal developments, so that they can perform their role as workplace representative armed with the facts.

1. Becoming a workplace representative

Whether you have just been appointed as a representative (this term includes shop stewards, workplace reps and office reps) for the first time, are a long standing representative who wants to make sure you are doing your best in your role, or just considering standing as a representative, then this section should offer you some useful advice on the functions of the representative and the law that might impact on these functions.

As a workplace representative you are, in law, an **official** of the union. The *Trade Union and Labour Relations (Consolidation) Act 1992* includes in the definition of an official:

> "a person elected or appointed in accordance with the rules of the union to be a representative of its members or of some of them, and includes a person so elected or appointed who is an employee of the same employer as the members or one or more of the members who he is to represent". (*section 119*)

Unions will have their own procedures covering the appointment or election of workplace representatives, but it is rare to find these detailed in the union rulebook.

For this booklet LRD surveyed the rulebooks of 29 TUC affiliated unions whose membership accounted for 76% of all TUC affiliates. Most unions had no specific rule covering workplace representatives. Nine unions did have rules and these are examined on pages 6 and 7.

The rules show that representatives may be asked to meet some **eligibility** test, usually to do with age, length of membership, or union activity. Whilst the law does not prescribe who can be a representative, these rules are designed to make sure that the representative has sufficient experience to carry out the tasks of the job and has sufficient knowledge of how the union operates.

Most unions will also have a rule or practice covering the **method of appointment** of the workplace representative. As a representative:

- you are likely to be elected by members in the workplace, usually at a specially convened meeting;
- this election is usually ratified at local, regional or national level, by a union body which may hand out credentials;
- you are likely to hold office for one or two years; and
- the body that ratifies appointment can withdraw ratification at any time.

According to the *1992 WIRS survey* elections are usually **by show of hands**, especially in the case of manual workers where 50%-60% of elections take place in this way, compared to 30%-50% for non-manuals. Very few unions use secret ballots to elect worker representatives. *WIRS* estimated that only one in four or one in five reps was elected by ballot.

There is **no legal requirement for ballots** for worker representatives' elections. The legislation on ballots for elections covers only general secretaries, union executives and other union officers with positions on national executive policy-making bodies.

Once appointed a representative needs to know what the role entails. Again a look at those unions with rules giving information on workplace representatives is a good place to start. From the box on pages 6 and 7 it can be seen that the **functions and duties** of workplace representatives can include the following:

- negotiating with the employer;
- recruiting new members;
- collecting union subscriptions;
- representing members in grievances and disciplinary hearings;
- reporting back to the union on workplace matters; and
- conveying information on union policies and activities back to the member.

Recognition

For a workplace representative to carry out the full range of duties, recognition is essential. A **recognition deal** is an agreement between the employer and the union that the employer will recognise the union as the competent authority over a range of issues which can include:

- individual representation;
- health and safety representation;
- consultation; and
- full negotiating rights.

Recognition deals that involve all or some of the first three issues are usually called **partial recognition** deals. For **full recognition** negotiating rights are essential.

There is, at present, no law which obliges an employer to recognise the union. Recognition can be granted and withdrawn on the employer's terms. However, there are some case law precedents which indicate the circumstances which can lead to a presumption of recognition. In one case, taken by the National Union of Tailors and Garment Workers (NUTGW) the judge ruled that

Union rules on worker representatives

A union that does have a rule covering workplace representatives is Manufacturing Science Finance (MSF). *Rule 40* states:
"For the purpose of furthering the interests and protecting the rights of members, workplace representatives must be established within each workplace where members are employed."

The general union GMB, in *Rule 45*, lays down the requirements for appointment or election of representatives and states that these are subject to the approval of the branch committee, or regional secretary if more than one branch is involved. Appointments can be by show of hands at the workplace or at a branch meeting or if by common consent, by regional appointment. Representatives appointed in this way are issued with a credential card, a badge and handbook.

The construction union UCATT states that the appointment of representatives must be in compliance with its *Rule 20*. Representatives are elected by a majority vote of members. Names of elected stewards are then forwarded to the regional secretary who issues the individual with an official steward's card. The steward has the task of checking if new recruits are qualified for the job they have been appointed to and also whether they are union members. Stewards also have to regularly check members' contributions cards. The steward also deals with local grievances and regularly meets the full-time officer.

The lock and metal workers' union is one of the smaller TUC affiliated unions which has a specific rule covering shop stewards. Under *Rule 27* stewards are elected at the workplace, but subject to executive committee approval. Stewards are responsible for making sure that members' contributions are up to date and are paid for their work.

Among non-manual workers the banking union, BIFU, has a rule (*Rule P*) which says that office representatives are elected or appointed in accordance with procedures laid down by the national executive and are responsible to the members who elect them. The functions of the representative are fivefold: to maintain contact with the union branch; to advise members on grievance or disciplinary procedures; to raise with management issues affecting office conditions; to communicate with members concerning union matters; and to recruit.

the fact that there was **no written agreement** was not essential to a finding that recognition had been granted. In a 1977 case, also taken by NUTGW (*NUTGW v Charles Ingram [1977] ICR 530*), recognition was inferred from the facts and the conduct of the employer over a period of time.

In a claim taken by shopworkers' union USDAW, evidence of recognition was deduced by collection of union dues with permission, consultation and the existence of a national agreement. But having the right to collect subs in isolation from other provisions does not amount to recognition according to the case of *USDAW v Sketchley [1981] IRLR 291*. Nor does a discussion about recognition amount to recognition itself (*TGWU v Andrew Dyer [1977] IRLR 93*).

The shopworkers' union USDAW, under *Rule 20* leaves it to union branches to decide if shop stewards are appointed. Members in the workplace nominate candidates who are elected at a workplace meeting. This election then has to be ratified by the branch. Once elected a shop steward holds office for two years. Stewards are directly responsible to the branch. To be eligible to stand a member must usually be aged over 18, have been a member for at least a year and attended at least half of all branch meetings. Once elected shop stewards may be responsible for collecting union subscriptions.

Unison, the largest UK union, covers the election and functions of stewards by rule. Stewards are elected on an annual basis by the members in the workplace. The election is ratified by the union branch which issues credentials. Stewards have five main responsibilities: to represent the interests of members at work, including grievances, discipline and negotiations; to establish and maintain union organisation, including convening meetings; to attend branch meetings; to report on all workplace developments; and to carry out their duties in line with the handbook issued to stewards.

At one time many unions would have had two types of representative, one known as the shop steward, the other being the "collecting steward". In the unions already referred to these roles have, in general, been merged, but in some unions the two are still separate. In the steel workers' union ISTC, for example, branch stewards can be appointed to collect subscriptions (*Rule 17*). Under *Rule 18*, a separate officer, the works representative takes on all other tasks of the rep, including local negotiations.

So far, in this examination of the rules affecting them, workplace representatives have been referred to under various titles including "representatives", "shop stewards", "office representatives" and "stewards". But there are other terms which have their origin in the particular industry or the sector they operate in. Chapel officers (including "mothers" and "fathers" of chapel), are still commonly found in the print industry. Despite this unusual term they perform the functions of the workplace representative. The journalists' union NUJ, under its *Rule 15*, says that the chapel is responsible: "for maintaining and extending union organisation"; ensuring that agreements are observed; and safeguarding members' interests. It is the chapel which elects the mother/father who is then responsible for negotiations. The rule also states that editors cannot serve as chapel officers.

At its 1995 Congress, the TUC called for specific legal rights to representation and negotiation. Congress adopted a document, *Your voice at work*, which proposes:

- a universal right to representation. This would be available to any worker requesting union representation on an individual issue, regardless of whether or not there was a formal union presence in the workplace;
- consultation rights, where 10% of employees are in the union with a fall-back position of a general consultation body where the employer refuses a union body; and
- trade union recognition where a majority vote for collective bargaining rights.

These proposals have been influenced by the requirements of European law and the need to aid in the development of **European works councils (EWCs)**. EWCs will be set up by companies with a significant number of employees in two or more European Union (EU) states. Although the UK government opted out of the requirement many UK companies are likely to set EWCs up and to involve UK workplace representatives in them.

The government has for its part introduced **new regulations** which it claims enact the requirements of a judgement of the European Court of Justice (ECJ) (see section 2). The regulations, effective from 1 March 1996, are intended to create a new layer of non-union representatives. The government's measures are significantly less wide-ranging than those of the TUC and, importantly, they actually involve a reduction of existing trade union rights (see page 16).

A recognition agreement is vital to the workplace representative. Although the agreement itself has no legal force, certain important legal rights only apply where the union has secured such a deal. Rights to consultation, disclosure of information, time off for union duties and activities cannot be triggered if the employer does not recognise the union.

Negotiating with the employer

The *WIRS* survey found that eight out of 10 representatives said that they were involved in meetings with management, whilst six out of 10 attended joint shop stewards meetings. Forty per cent (four out of 10) said that they attended combine meetings or some other form of meeting with other union representatives. Those who went to combine meetings found that they were attending a meeting on average every three months and in about one in three workplaces management contributed to the cost of these meetings.

It is usually presumed that **agreements** concluded between union representatives and management will be **binding** on individual employees whose contracts customarily change through collective bargaining. The agreement can be incorporated into an employee's contract **"expressly"**, in other words the contract may actually state that the changes to it will take place in accordance with the collective agreement. But changes can also be **"implied"**. This happens where it has been customary for contracts to change in this way.

Where there is evidence of neither express nor implied incorporation the courts have, in a few rare cases, been prepared to rule that the union representative had concluded the agreement as an **"agent"** of the employees. In the case of *Lee v GEC Plessey Telecommunications [1993] IRLR 383* the employer tried to defeat an employees' claim for enhanced redundancy pay on the grounds that the union representative had agreed to withdraw from litigation. The High Court held that the union was **not acting as an agent** of the employees as it was not authorised to settle litigation on the employees' behalf.

In workplaces where the union is recognised (see page 5 for what this means), then there is a legal **right to be paid** while carrying out trade union duties (and these include the duties of worker representatives). Section three deals with the law on time off for union duties and on payment. Some unions also provide for payment where there is no recognition agreement. The general union, GMB, for example, has a rule which allows the branch to establish a levy to pay loss of earnings to shop stewards where their employer does not pay. The locksmiths' union NULMW remunerates shop stewards for their services under a rule which allows the executive council to set a rate.

Workplace representatives may find that they are involved in new consultative machinery once **European Works Councils (EWCs)** are firmly established (see page 8). Some workplace representatives will find themselves directly involved in the formation of the new EWCs and will sit on them as representatives of the whole workforce from each European Union state where company employees are situated.

Recruiting members and collecting subs

Many representatives now also act as recruitment and collecting stewards, responsible for getting in contributions in workplaces not on check-off (that is not having union subscriptions deducted out of your pay) or where the member has not gone on to direct debit. Recruiting members is undoubtedly a job that requires enthusiasm, an ability to listen to what non-members are saying and an even more essential ability of explaining to workers why trade union membership is important for them.

Many have argued that representatives had lost some of these skills in the period when 100% membership deals were on offer and it often seemed that it was left up to the employer to let new recruits know about the union. But since 1994, with the change in the law brought about under *section 15* of the *Trade Union Reform and Employment Rights Act 1993*, workplace representatives have had to play a leading role in persuading members to re-sign. The law now requires unions, every three years, to get a member's written approval that they want to remain in the union. Without representatives in the workplace, this would become an extremely difficult exercise.

If an individual claims that union contributions are being deducted from salary without authorization, the workplace representative is **not legally liable**. *Section 15* makes it clear that it is the employer who has to ensure that every deduction made is authorised and a worker who complains of an unauthorised deduction takes the complaint against the employer.

A number of unions now offer **direct debit** facilities. These get over the danger of employers threatening to withdraw check-off (as the railway employers did during the recent train drivers' industrial action). Members paying by direct debit do not come under the *section 15* requirements, including those relating to re-signing.

Representing members

An important element of the day to day work of a representative is in representing individual members in **grievance** or **disciplinary** matters. To carry out this role a representative needs to be reasonably familiar with the legal rules, particularly in disciplinary matters. It is important that representatives give accurate advice, especially when it concerns a member's legal rights.

If a representative gives a member **incorrect advice**, say over the time limits for submitting tribunal applications or fails to apply for a protective award in redundancy cases when one should have been obtained, then the member would have grounds for a claim of negligence against the union itself. The workplace representative would be acting in the capacity of an official of the union and is therefore likely to escape personal liability.

The House of Lords decided in the case of *Heatons Transport (St Helens) v TGWU [1972] IRLR 25* that the **union was liable** for the action of its shop stewards. The Law Lords suggested that there was an implied authority given to the shop stewards by the union.

Nevertheless, the possibility of **negligence claims** makes it important that no advice is given on legal rights unless it has been fully checked by someone competent to give the advice (like the union's solicitor) or sufficiently knowledgable of the legal issues and rules.

In the case of *Cross v BISKTA [1968] Weekly Law Reports (WLR) 494* the Court of Appeal was asked to rule in a negligence claim where the union had submitted a member's personal injury claim to the solicitor but, on the solicitor's advice, had not pur-

sued the claim. Lord Justice Salmon, delivering the court's judgement, said that the responsibilities of the local representative (in that case the branch secretary) were limited to obtaining from the member the full particulars of the accident and passing them on to the solicitors. Acting on the solicitor's advice meant that the union could not be sued for negligence.

In the case of *Times Newspapers v O'Regan [1977] IRLR 101* Ms O'Regan submitted her unfair dismissal application out of time because her union rep had told her that the three month time limit ran from the date when negotiations on her case ended. In giving judgement against her application to have the time limit extended, the Employment Appeal Tribunal (EAT) pointed out that **relying on bad advice** was not a defence for ignoring the time limit (she should have checked with a competent authority). However, the EAT left open the question of whether she could indeed have sued the union for having given her the bad advice.

The courts are also unwilling to uphold a complaint by an individual member that the union has not served the member's interests well. In the case of *Oddy v TSSA [1973] ICR 524* the court ruled that a union's refusal to represent an individual in a grievance against the employer did not give grounds for a case against the union official.

This principle of the law remaining outside the issue of union service provision was confirmed in the case of *Iwanuszezak v GMB [1988] IRLR 219*. The facts were as follows:

> Geoffrey Iwanuszezak was made redundant following a negotiated change to shift patterns which meant he could not work due to poor eyesight. He brought a negli-

gence claim against the union alleging that the union had failed in its duty of care to him. The Court of Appeal rejected the claim.

Lord Justice Lloyd stated:

> "the primary function of a union is to look after the collective interests of its members. When the collective interests of the union conflict with the interests of an individual member, it only makes sense that the collective interests of the members as a whole should prevail."

Reporting back

Worker representatives are an important channel of two-way communication between the union and its members. Under their rules many unions require workplace representatives to inform members of union policy and to act in accordance with that policy. Representatives can also be a way of letting the union know the views of the membership. This can be done either by attending regularly the union branch or district meetings or through regular meetings of all workplace representatives in a particular area or industry.

Some of these meetings will be in working time and the arrangements highlighted in section 3 of this booklet explain the law on paid time off.

2. Information and consultation rights

As a workplace representative in a recognised workplace you have specific rights to information for collective bargaining purposes and to be consulted over issues of redundancy or business transfers, although your consultation rights may be more limited as the result of a recent change in the law (see page 16).

Information for collective bargaining

Section 181 of the *Trade Union and Labour Relations (Consolidation) Act 1992* imposes a general duty on an employer, who recognises an independent trade union, to disclose to representatives of the union on request, information which the employer, or an associated employer has:

> "(a) without which the trade union representative would be to a material extent impeded in carrying on collective bargaining with him, and
> (b) which would be in accordance with **good industrial relations practice** that he should disclose to them for the purposes of collective bargaining".

The union should give the employer the **names** of the reps authorised to carry out collective bargaining. In multi-union sites unions should try to co-ordinate their requests for information. The employer can ask for the request to be in **writing** and representatives should be as precise as possible about the nature of the information they want.

According to the *WIRS* survey one in five manual worker representatives have used the law to get rights to information, as have one in eight non-manual worker reps.

Section 181 is supplemented by an ACAS *Code of Practice: Disclosure of Information to Trade Unions for Collective Bargaining Purposes (1977)*. This says that providing information which "would influence the formulation, presentation or pursuance of a claim or the conclusion of an agreement" accords with good industrial relations practice (*para 9*).

The code also gives examples of the kind of information which could be relevant, and while making it clear that the list is not exhaustive, the code says that information on:

- pay and benefits;
- conditions of service;
- staffing;
- performance; and
- financial matters

would fall within the general remit of relevant information.

Section 181 is limited, to some extent, by *section 182* of the same Act. This absolves an employer of the duty to disclose information on the grounds of national security, or where the employer obtained it in confidence or where its release could cause substantial injury to the business.

The Code says that the employer is not obliged to produce original documents or to compile information which would entail work disproportionate to the benefit which representatives could derive from having it.

The Code says (*para 20*) that employers should be "as open and helpful as possible" and make information available as soon as possible. They should present information in an understandable form and should explain why information cannot be provided when this happens.

If an employer refuses to comply with a request for information then the union can complain to the **Central Arbitration Committee (CAC)**. The CAC is an independent standing arbitration body working nationally in industrial relations. One of its tasks is to adjudicate on claims over disclosure of information.

The CAC can make a finding that obliges the employer to release the information. However, on the basis of the case of *R v CAC ex parte Tioxide [1982] IRLR 60* it cannot make an award outside the area for which the union has recognition rights. In the Tioxide case the union had **limited bargaining rights**. When it tried to get information on a job evaluation scheme which it did not bargain over the High Court ruled that the law did not give it the right to request that type of information.

However, where employers have negotiated by custom and practice they cannot bypass their obligation to provide information simply by declaring that they will not bargain on a particular occasion, according to the recent CAC award in *HM Prisons and the POA (CAC award 95/1)*. The facts were as follows:

> The union had requested information on market testing and the employer refused to give it. The CAC accepted that there was no intention on the part of the employer to collectively bargain over market testing but even without this intent the CAC made an award in favour of the union.

The chair of the CAC said that *section 181* was "intended to indicate the duty to supply information arises wherever there is a recognised practice of collective bargaining on the issue in question". If this were not the case then employers could avoid their obligation to disclose information just by announcing, in any given situation, that they had decided not to negotiate.

The the CAC decision makes it clear that where there is a **custom of bargaining** then the employer will be bound by the *section 181* provisions.

Other awards made by the CAC include one to oblige employers to give the union information on the distribution of percentage pay awards across certain staff groups where the union needed the information to assess a new performance pay system (*General Accident and MSF/APEX (1989)*).

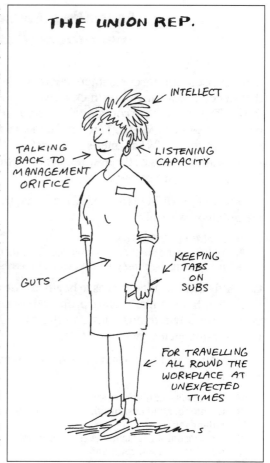

THE UNION REP.

INTELLECT

TALKING BACK TO MANAGEMENT ORIFICE

LISTENING CAPACITY

GUTS

KEEPING TABS ON SUBS

FOR TRAVELLING ALL ROUND THE WORKPLACE AT UNEXPECTED TIMES

The CAC in its 1993 report pointed out that unions find annual pay negotiations "a fertile ground" for disputes over disclosure of information. It said that particular difficulties arise where the pay of some people is individually assessed. Although the report said that it would not order an employer to provide information which identifies individuals, its view is "that some broad information should be disclosed" in such cases.

Other areas where information disclosure provisions have been referred to the CAC include, in 1994, market testing and terms and conditions of employment and, in 1993, grading schemes not jointly agreed and privatisation. Trade union representatives facing privatisation could consider using *section 181*.

Consulting the union — the current situation

A recognised union representative has the legal right to be consulted over threatened redundancies or in cases where the business is likely to be transferred. These rights are contained in *section 188 TULR(C)A 1992* as amended by *section 34 TURERA 1993* (redundancies) and in the *Transfer of Undertakings Regulations 1981* as amended by *section 33 TURERA 1993*. These requirements will change once the new regulations, effective from 1 March 1996, come into operation (see below).

Section 188 TURERA (as amended) says that the employer has to consult with the union on ways of:

- **avoiding** the dismissals;
- **reducing** the numbers of employees to be dismissed; and
- **mitigating** the consequences of the dismissals.

Currently this consultation has to begin "**at the earliest opportunity**". Where more than 10 redundancies are proposed consultation should begin at least 30 days before any redundancies, and this period rises to 90 days where 100 or more redundancies are contemplated.

In the course of the consultation the employer is required to "**disclose in writing**":

- the reasons for his proposal;
- the number and descriptions of employees whom it is proposed to dismiss as redundant;
- the total number of employees at the establishment;
- the method of selection; and
- the proposed method of carrying out the dismissals.

Consultation involves the employer **considering representations** made by the union and **replying** to them.

Under *Regulation 10* of the *Transfer of Undertakings (Protection of Employment) Regulations 1981 (TUPE)* employers must inform representatives "long enough before the relevant transfer": of the fact that it is taking place, when it is taking place and the reasons for it; of the legal, economic and social implications of the transfer; and of the measures envisaged to be taken in relation to employees. The employer has to consult with any recognised unions (with a view to reaching agreement) and has to consider any representations made by the representatives and reply stating the reasons for any rejection.

Changes in 1996

The above describes the main rights trade union representatives have had to be consulted. The government has produced **new regulations** which have an impact on trade union consultation rights.

The *Collective Redundancies and Transfer of Undertakings (Protection of Employment) (Amendment) Regulation 1995*, come into force on 1 March 1996, as far as provisions relating to consultation are concerned. They remove the requirement to consult in cases where fewer than 20 redundancies are being contemplated within a 90 day period. Under *TULR(C)A 1992* no minimum number was specified and the courts had ruled that the employer should consult even where only one employee was being made redundant.

The second main change in the regulations is that the requirement to consult "at the earliest opportunity", is amended to a requirement to consult "in good time". This may be interpreted to permit employers to begin consultations later than under the 1992 provisions. Certainly the government has described the change as "more realistic" than the existing requirement.

The most significant change to come from the new regulations, however, concerns the **rights of union representatives themselves**. The regulations remove the obligation to consult with the union's reps replacing this with an obligation to consult either with union reps or with **specially appointed representatives**. These new representatives do not need to be approved by the union, even in recognised workplaces. Nor would they be permanently appointed representatives.

The regulations envisage situations where representatives would be appointed from the employees affected and recognised purely during the period of consultation. Once the redundancy or business transfer had taken place then these new reps lose their rights to be consulted.

When the government first brought forward these proposals (which it did very surreptitiously in April 1995) it claimed that they met the standards set by European law and by the judges of the European Court of Justice, which had declared existing UK consultation rights inadequate and in breach of European directives.

There is grave doubt among leading lawyers about the adequacy of the government's new proposals. Lord Wedderburn, a prominent lawyer specialising in employment law, has advised the TUC that a non-permanent body of worker representatives is unlikely to meet the standards of independence (from the employer) required by EU law.

The regulations **are defective** in many other ways. They are unclear as to how these new reps would be appointed and who would set off the process for their nomination. It is also not clear how the courts would view a situation where an employer was consulting with "tame reps", appointed on a temporary basis, while the workforce as a whole made it clear that it considered its permanent trade union representatives as the only legitimate reps.

For all these reasons existing trade union representatives should continue to **insist that employers consult** with them, pointing out to employers that there are likely to be legal challenges to the new regulations and that there are strong arguments suggesting they are an inadequate attempt to comply with European law.

Of course, the majority of employers who have recognised unions are unlikely to want to suddenly begin consulting with non-union groups because of the harm that this would do to industrial relations in the workplace as well as increasing the risk of legal challenges. The rest of this section of the booklet examines the case law on consultation from the perspective of its application as a trade union right.

"At the earliest opportunity"

As has been noted *section 188* requires that employers consult "at the earliest opportunity". This term has been interpreted in a number of cases before the courts. In *Hough v Leyland DAF [1991] IRLR 194* the judges decided that employers had to consult with the union once matters had reached a stage where there has been a specific proposal. This was a stage which was later than when a problem had been diagnosed but earlier than when a recommendation to proceed with redundancies has been reached.

As was noted on page 17, the requirement for consultation "at the earliest opportunity" will be amended for one of consultation "in good time".

> ## *Meaningful consultation*

The law requires the employer to enter into meaningful consultation. In the case of *MSF v GEC Ferranti (Defence Systems) [1994] IRLR 113* the EAT said that this meant that the employer had to provide adequate information. Although it did not mean the employer had to provide precise details on jobs and numbers, it was certainly not sufficient to do what GEC Ferranti had done which was to give the union a copy of the legal notice which it had sent to the

Employment Department. (Employers now send this to the DTI following the abolition of the Employment Department.)

The requirement to consult is also a requirement in European law, under the *Collective Redundancies Directive 75/129*. In the case of *R v British Coal Corporation and Secretary of State for Trade and Industry ex parte Vardy [1993] IRLR 104*, a case concerning redundancy procedures in the coal industry, Mr Justice Glidewell said that the Directive required the employer to consult on ways of avoiding redundancies, by not closing the particular establishment, if that is what the employer had in mind.

The fact that consultation should be meaningful does not mean that the employer has to accept the union point of view. As long as the union is given a fair and proper opportunity to understand fully the issues, and the employer considers the union's views genuinely and properly, then this amounts to fair consultation according to the case of *R v British Coal Corporation and Sec of State ex part Price [1994] IRLR 72*.

Members involved

According to the recent case of *Governing Body of the Northern Ireland Hotel and Catering College v NATFHE [1995] IRLR 83* employers must consult with **all recognised unions** which have members in the grades of those likely to be made redundant, even if the employer's proposals for redundancies do not involve members of some recognised unions. In the NATFHE case the employer had consulted only with the union whose members were being targeted for redundancy. NATFHE, as a recognised union for the grade of staff, successfully argued that it too should have been consulted.

3. Carrying out trade union duties effectively

As the WIRS survey makes clear, granting facilities to workplace representatives and giving them the necessary time off to undertake their duties "are indications of the degree of support that a local management gives to workplace trade unionism". But they are also indicators of the level of support for the union in the workplace. The same WIRS survey found that management is less likely to provide facilities and adequate time off in workplaces with low levels of union membership.

As a workplace representative and an official of an independent, recognised union you have the right, under *section 168* of the *Trade Union and Labour Relations (Consolidation) Act 1992*, to have paid time off during working hours to carry out your union duties. You also have the right to paid time off for **training** to carry out your duties, provided the training is TUC approved, or approved by your union and is concerned with collective bargaining (see page 21).

The law does not give an unlimited right to time off, as *section 168* is qualified by the words "reasonable in all the circumstances". This permits employers to refuse time off provided that they are acting reasonably in doing so.

You do not have to have worked for a specific length of time before getting time off provided you are an accredited workplace representative, although some union rules (see pages 6 and 7) require a prospective representative to have worked for a specific period or been a union member for a specified period.

Trade union duties

If there already is an established system of representation in your workplace, then there may be an agreement, or understanding, about the type of duties for which you have the right to paid time off. The agreement may define these duties in some detail. An LRD survey, published in the magazine *Bargaining Report* (July 1994), found that 40% of respondents had a written agreement. The reason why many did not was that they had been in well organised workplaces where procedures had operated smoothly for a considerable period of time.

Section 168 of the *1992 Act* also gives a definition of trade union duties and, as a minimum, any agreement with the employer should take account of this and therefore should include:

- duties connected with negotiations related to or concerning **collective bargaining;** and
- any other agreed duties.

Collective bargaining is itself defined in *section 178(2)* and includes: terms and conditions; hiring, firing and suspension; allocation of work; discipline; trade union membership; facilities; and the machinery for negotiation and consultation.

Trade union duties can, of course, extend beyond the definition in *section 168* to include informing members about negotiations or consultations, meeting with lay and full-time officials, interviewing and meeting with members to discuss disciplinary or grievance issues; representing members at industrial tribunals; and explaining to new recruits how the union functions.

An ACAS *Code of practice on time off for trade union duties (1991)* gives guidance on how the law should be interpreted. It recommends a formal agreement between the employer and the union. It also says that the employer should take account of the particular difficulties of individual representatives or of those representing shift workers.

Facilities at work

To perform the job of a workplace representative effectively most trade unionists find that they need access to certain facilities, like a telephone, office and possibly computer equipment. The WIRS survey says that the effectiveness of individual reps is partly dependent on the range and quality of facilities they receive. The law does not lay down the kind of facilities your employer should make available. However, the code of practice states that

"where resources permit the facilities could include:
- accommodation for meetings;
- access to a telephone and other office equipment;
- the use of notice boards;
- when the volume of the official's work justifies it, the use of a dedicated office space". *(para 28)*

A facilities agreement, concluded between employer and the union, could provide for all or some of these facilities. It should also be remembered that although the code of practice does not have the same status as legislation, a tribunal can take account of its content when deciding whether the employer acted reasonably.

As many as three in four reps will have access to a telephone and more than half (75% of non-manuals) will have access to a computer (or typewriter) according to the WIRS survey. Fewer had faxes (the survey was carried out in 1990 and the figures are likely to be higher now) but at least one in four manual reps and nearly half all non-manuals could get access to a fax at work.

There have been few cases before the tribunals on the issue of facilities. But in the House of Lords ruling in the case of *Post Office v Crouch [1974] IRLR 22* the judges ruled that denying an unrecognised union the right to organise activities on works premises outside working hours was action short of dismissal taken for the purpose of preventing or deterring trade union membership.

Trade union training

"Trade union officials are more likely to carry out their duties effectively if they possess skills and knowledge relevant to their duties" (*para 18 Code of practice*). Trade unions offer a vast range of specialist training courses for worker representatives and the law says that a representative has the right to time off with pay to attend training. Under *section 168 TULR(C)A 1992*

"training in aspects of industrial relations –
■ relevant to the carrying out of duties; and
■ approved by the TUC or by the independent union of which he is an official
should be permitted".

The WIRS survey found that in 37% of workplaces some reps had been trained in the preceding year. This was usually provided by the union in working time.

The *Code of practice* says that there is "no one recommended syllabus for training" but that these will vary according to the collective bargaining arrangements, the union structure and the role of the official. It recommends that employers release representatives for **initial training** on representation skills "as soon as possible after their election or appointment". Further training should be made available:

■ for officials with **specific responsibilities**;
■ where there are proposals to **change the structure or topics of negotiation**;
■ where significant **changes in the workplace** are contemplated; or
■ where **legislation** could have an impact on industrial relations.

The training has to be appropriate to the representative. In one case, *MOD v Crook and Irving [1982] IRLR 488*, the EAT said that since a union course was described as for convenors and senior stewards it was reasonable for the employer to refuse ordinary shop stewards permission to attend .

The right to payment for time off for training is limited to the hours when the representative would have been at work had it not been for the training.

In the case of *Hairsine v Kingston-upon-Hull City Council [1992] IRLR 211* the EAT said that a representative who was a shiftworker working afternoons and evenings could only claim payment for the part of the course which took place during his normal working hours.

Somewhat in contrast to this ruling is a 1992 ruling of the European Court of Justice in a case brought by a staff representative, Ms Botel. She was a part-time worker but when she attended a full-time training course she was able to argue successfully that denying her the right to be paid the same rate as applied to full time workers was indirect discrimination which the employer had to justify.

These rights to training have been further defined by the judges who have ruled that there may be circumstances where even an item over which there is no negotiation, (like a pension scheme), could be appropriate for time off for training (*Menzies v Smith and McLaurin [1980] IRLR 180*).

What you get paid

You have the right to be paid at your normal rate of pay excluding any voluntary (but not contractual) overtime.

Examples of where trade union representatives have been able to secure time off with pay include:

■ attendance at a meeting of representatives to prepare for collective negotiations with the employer (*London Ambulance Service v Charlton [1992] IRLR 510*); and
■ attending a delegate conference to consider recommendations for industrial action (*Oxford and County Newspapers v McIntyre (unreported) 1986*).

If your employer grants time off but then proposes to pay just for part of this time a tribunal is likely to view the employer's action as unfair.

If you are not given time off, or are not paid for the time off you have taken you can appeal to an industrial tribunal within three months of the refusal of the request or the payment. Under *section 172(1)* a tribunal may award compensation and can make a declaration as to your entitlement to time off. In most cases the remedy is limited to the declaration.

Can an employer refuse time off?

Not every request for time off has to be granted as the law only requires an employer to act reasonably in responding to time off requests. This means that requests can be refused. One situation where a refusal might occur is where the request for time off is at short notice. It is important to try to give the employer as much advance notice of your time off requirements as this prevents the employer from asserting that it would not be unreasonable to turn the request down.

However, some employers have been refusing time off as a matter of principle, or tightening up on the conditions under which time off is conceded. The *Bargaining Report* survey found that 30% of those replying were experiencing difficulty in getting time off and 10% had difficulty in getting time off for training because their employer deemed it not to be appropriate.

Difficulties also arise where workforce reductions put increased pressure on remaining staff so that it is harder to get time off. Using the law to challenge these refusals can be useful in forcing employers to concede requests for time off.

In one tribunal case a representative who had recently completed one training course was refused permission to attend another on the same subject and the tribunal said that this was reasonable. In the case of *Allen & Others v Thomas Scott and Sons (Bakers) [1983] IRLR 329* the Court of Appeal held that a request to attend a union meeting to discuss the industry's agreement on the busiest day of the week was unreasonable. Similarly a refusal to concede a request that all representatives attend a training course at the same time is likely to be upheld as reasonable.

In the *Hairsine* case (see page 23) the EAT did state that reasonable practice would have involved the employer and union jointly agreeing suitable arrangements for time off. This could involve minimising an employee's absence from work where possible. The EAT also went on to say that a reasonable employer might consider giving night shift workers time off between the end of their training course and the start of a new shift.

A blanket decision to refuse all time off for financial reasons could also be unreasonable. In the case of *Gething v Hampshire CC (unreported 1985)*, the tribunal said that the fact that the employers had not considered the merits of the particular representative's application made their refusal unreasonable.

4. Industrial disputes in the workplace

As a workplace representative you are likely to be faced with industrial disputes which may lead to calling or organising industrial action. Although it is likely that your union rule book will require authorization of strike action from a higher union authority, there are a number of issues which workplace representatives will need to deal with and this will require a knowledge of the relevant law. The main concerns of workplace representatives are:

- what their rights are to time off;
- whether they are personally liable for damages caused by the action;
- in what way the union is liable for what they do;
- what the ballot requirements are, and the steps they should take;
- does it matter whether the dispute is official or unofficial; and
- involvement in other disputes.

Time off to deal with disputes

When a dispute arises at work representatives are often faced with a considerable amount of additional work. Members have to be consulted and advised at every stage of the procedures or negotiations and unions usually have to be kept informed about all developments. Section 3 of the booklet explained the legal rights to time off which workplace representatives are entitled to. Where there is an agreed time off procedure it should take account of factors like additional meetings in periods of dispute. The *code of practice on time off* recognises that:

> "Employers and unions have a responsibility to use agreed procedures to settle problems and avoid industrial action. Time off may therefore be permitted for this purpose, particularly where there is a dispute" (*para 30*).

These time off provisions apply in the period before industrial action commences. There is no legal right to time off, either paid or unpaid, to take industrial action. *Section 170(2) TULR(C)A 1992* makes it clear that trade union "activities" for which unpaid time off is available under the law, does not extend to:

> "activities which themselves consist of industrial action, whether or not in contemplation or furtherance of a trade dispute".

The one **exception** to this rule is where a representative is not personally taking part in industrial action but represents members involved. *Para 30* of the *Code of Practice on time off* also says:

> "where an official (including a workplace representative) is not taking part in industrial action but represents members involved, normal arrangements for time off with pay for the official should apply".

What these different provisions mean is that you should:

■ get paid time off for negotiations in the context of a dispute;
■ get paid time off to report to your members on the outcome of negotiations;
■ get paid time off to represent members taking industrial action where you are not a party to that action; but
■ have no entitlement to time off paid or unpaid, while yourself taking industrial action.

Personal liability

Despite the fact that you are the union representative it is unlikely that you will be held to be liable in law for your members' strike action. In the UK there is no "right to strike" as is the case in most other industrialised countries and trade unions are protected from the legal consequences of taking strike action through the system of "immunities". These state that, provided all the rules for lawful action (including ballots) have been complied with then the union's funds are protected from claims for damages. Workplace representatives have the same protection under the immunities in respect of inducing breaches of contract. By calling or supporting lawful industrial action you are not risking a challenge to your personal resources or liberty.

However, worker representatives can have legal action taken against them for their own breach of contract but this is a risk which they share equally with all other employees because every time a worker takes strike action they are breaching their contracts (an unlawful act) and could be sued by their employer. The reality, however, is that it is exceptionally rare for an employer to take employees to court in this way.

Union liability

When representatives organise or call industrial action they are taking this action on the union's behalf (unless the union repudiates the action). *Section 20(2) TULR(C)A 1992* says that an action "shall be taken to have been authorised or endorsed by a trade union" if it was done by "any other committee of the union or any other official of the union (whether employed by it or not)" and a "committee" is defined as "a group of persons constituted in accordance with the rules".

The effect of this provision is to bring workplace representatives and workplace committees within the authorization of the union unless repudiated. Any action undertaken by workplace representatives or committees in that capacity is deemed to be authorised unless the union repudiates. This means that liability falls on the union, not on the individual worker representative.

This principle was established as long ago as 1972 in the case of *Heatons Transport v TGWU [1972] IRLR 25* when the House of Lords held that shop stewards had authority, not only to negotiate, but also to take industrial action so making the union liable. The Lords made this ruling (reversing an earlier Court of Appeal ruling) to secure the release of five shop stewards who had been imprisoned.

The impact of the ruling was to make it very unlikely that employers would move against individual worker representatives in the future. No doubt the Court was guided in its decision by the mass spontaneous strike which had greeted the imprisonment of the five, an outcome which clearly the Law Lords did not wish to see repeated.

The union will also be liable even where it has seemingly distanced itself from particular strike action if its officials continue to support it (*Express and Star v NGA & Lowe [1986] unreported*). Again in the case of *Richard Read (Transport) v NUM (S. Wales) [1985] IRLR 67* a case arising from the 1984/85 miners' dispute, the Court ruled that the fact that the union had not expressly called for various types of action on the picket line did not mean that the union was not liable.

Ballots and the law

To benefit from the "immunities" trade unions need to have organised a ballot before any industrial action begins. In most unions now responsibility for organisation of ballots is done centrally and representatives may not necessarily be involved in the process, once a decision to ballot has been taken. For this reason the booklet deals only in brief with the law on ballots. The list below shows the main requirements which must be followed if the ballot is to be valid. Representatives should, however, be aware of the fact that this is an area where the law is continually in flux, as new court rulings place additional requirements on trade unions.

Ballots: what representatives need to know

To comply with the legal rules you must:

■ have a secret, postal ballot with the ballot form sent to the member's nominated address. A show of hands or workplace ballot is not enough;
■ your employer has to be told that a ballot is to take place at least seven days before the papers go out and must be given three days' notice of its content; a further two stages of notification involve giving the employer the result and seven days' notice of any action;
■ have appointed an independent scrutineer to handle the voting process;
■ ask a specific question on the ballot paper requiring members to answer yes or no to strike action, or action short of a strike and must include a statement on strike action and breach of contract;
■ ensure that action commences within four weeks of the last date for voting; and
■ you must indicate who will be called on to take industrial action either by calling out those whom the employer can identify or by providing a list of the names of those who are to be called out.

(For more detail on the law and ballots see LRD's booklet *The Law at Work, 1994*)

You are free to **campaign for a "yes" vote** and you do not risk legal action merely for doing this.

Official and unofficial disputes

An "official" dispute is any dispute which the union has not repudiated. A dispute only becomes "unofficial" where repudiation has taken place. The effect of this wide definition of "official" disputes is to guarantee that liability falls on the union not the individual representative. If you are involved in organising an official dispute then it is likely that any action for damages or injunction to prevent the dispute will be issued against the union itself.

If the dispute is unofficial and the union has repudiated the strike by sending out notices to members that it is not calling or supporting the action then, as a workplace representative, you could face three specific legal actions:

1) You may be **named on an application** for an injunction taken out by the employer to prevent the strike. If this occurs you can of course obey the injunction and not call on your members to take industrial action (the fact that they might continue in the stoppage does not necessarily put you in contempt of court). In the Timex Dundee dispute, in 1993, the convenor and deputy convenor had injunctions issued against them. The interdicts (injunctions) called on the named officials to refrain from organising picketing. Although

the injunctions lasted for the duration of the dispute, picketing did still continue.

A refusal to comply with an injunction puts those named at risk of contempt of court proceedings.

In an analysis of 156 injunctions initiated by employers between 1980 and 1994, LRD found that fewer than five could be identified as having been taken against individual workers. In one case in 1988 British Rail secured an injunction against five ASLEF reps ordering them to withdraw the instruction for secondary action and not to call further strikes; in 1990 Shell UK was granted an injunction against individual offshore workers taking part in a sit-in, and in 1993 came the Timex injunction to which reference has already been made.

2. You could face **selective dismissal**. This is equally a risk faced by all other strikers taking unofficial action, but the fact that the law permits the employer to target individual workers taking unofficial action can give employers an opportunity to get rid of workplace representatives.

3. You could face an **action for damages** from the employer.

In reality, although employers may be willing to pursue injunctions against workplace representatives in cases of unofficial action, they are very unlikely to pursue an action for damages. The main reason for this is that they have to assess the extent of the damage occasioned by the individual worker.

This was graphically revealed in the 1958 case of *National Coal Board v Galley [1958] I Weekly Law Reports 16*. The Coal Board tried to claim damages from Mr Galley because he had breached his contract by taking industrial action. However, the employer was unable to quantify exactly how much lost production was attributable to Mr Galley personally and in the end the claim collapsed.

The view that pursuing individuals in damages claims was inappropriate reasserted itself in the case of *NWL Ltd v Woods [1979] ICR 867*. There the employers had applied for an injunction against named officials. In deciding to grant the injunction Lord Diplock, in the House of Lords pointed out that the injunction was the only appropriate remedy because:

> "if it (the injunction) is not granted and the action against him ultimately succeeds it is most improbable that damages on the scale that are likely to be awarded against him will prove recoverable from him".

What the judge was pointing out was that it was pointless pursuing damages' claims from worker representatives who would never have the assets to meet the claim. The judge also pointed out that by the time a full damages claim could get to the courts, months after the industrial action:

"it would not be in the employer's interest to exacerbate relations with the workmen by continuing proceedings against the individual defendants none of whom would be capable financially of meeting a substantial claim for damages".

And he pointed out that any damages which could be recovered "would be very small".

Getting involved in other disputes

The legal changes of the 1980s and beyond have effectively outlawed all forms of secondary action. But workplace representatives may find occasionally that they are involved in industrial action not directly related to their own working terms and conditions. For example, as a representative you could be responsible for a number of different work sections. If one of these (not the one you actually work in) wants to take industrial action you need to know what your rights are.

Under *section 220* of the *Trade Union and Labour Relations (Consolidation) Act 1992 (TULR(C)A)* an "official" of a union (the definition includes workplace reps – see page 4) can picket "at or near the place of work" of members whom the rep is accompanying and whom she/he represents. This gives representatives the right to join their members on picket lines without the risk of opening up themselves or the union to damages claims.

5. Victimisation

As a trade union representative you are protected from employer victimisation because of your duties or activities. *Section 146* of the *Trade Union and Labour Relations (Consolidation) Act 1992 (TULR(C)A)* says that employees have "the right not to have action short of dismissal" taken against them aimed at "deterring or preventing them from taking part in union activities". *Section 152* of the same Act protects against dismissal on similar grounds, and *Section 137* similarly protects applicants for employment.

The law protects all union members, but it is union representatives in the workplace who are more likely to need its protection and many of the cases interpreting the law have been pursued by workplace representatives.

This section explains how these legal interpretations and, in particular, some recent judgements, have guaranteed protection and then looks at a specific procedure – **interim relief** – available in cases of dismissal.

Activities prior to employment

It has been well established through a number of cases that it is unfair to victimise someone on the grounds of their previous trade union activities. A workplace representative who goes to work elsewhere can claim automatic unfair dismissal if the employer's actions are in response to information about past union activities. The leading case on this issue is the decision of the Court of Appeal in *Fitzpatrick v BRB [1991] IRLR 376*. The facts were as follows:

> Denise Fitzpatrick was employed by British Rail. Six months later she was dismissed and the reasons given by her employer were that she had failed to disclose details of all her past employment record which included a job from which she had been dismissed on account of trade union activities.

The Court of Appeal held that she had been dismissed because her employers believed that she would take part in trade union activities. This meant that her dismissal did fall within *Section 152* of the 1992 Act.

Carrying out union duties

The protection extends to all your union duties and these do not have to be duties which the employer approves of so long as they are being carried out

32   LRD

under the time off agreement. The Court of Appeal case of *Burgess v Bass Taverns (1995) IDSB 548* demonstrates clearly how this rule operates.

ABOVE : THE LAST EMPLOYER WHO TRIED TO VICTIMISE A UNION REP WITHOUT KNOWING WHAT HER RIGHTS WERE.

Burgess was a senior member of staff but also the union rep. At a union presentation for new employees he stated that when it came to industrial injuries "it will be the union who fights for you not the company". For making this statement the company dismissed him on the grounds that he was not displaying the loyalty expected of senior employees.

The Court rejected the employer's case and upheld the right of union representatives to comment on the performance of the company, except where the comments were motivated by malice or dishonesty. The Court said that it was "unrealistic" to expect union reps to use a union meeting merely to promote harmonious relations with the employer.

Similarly, a threat to discipline a union representative because she had given a press comment about her union's affairs could come within the *Section 146* definition according to the case of *British Airways Engine Overhaul v Francis [1981] IRLR 9.*

Action short of dismissal

Many representatives in workplaces where the employer seems to reluctantly accept the union, report action taken against them to deter them from union activities. This can involve a range of measures taken by the employer including a **transfer** to other work. This was what occurred in the case of *Robb v Leon Motor Services [1978] IRLR 26.*

Mr Robb was a driver and was appointed shop steward at his depot. The company transferred him to another site. The tribunal found that the transfer was specifically designed to isolate him from the workers he represented, because the company felt that he approached his union duties with too much enthusiasm.

At the EAT Robb argued successfully that the transfer did amount to "action short of dismissal" taken to prevent his union activities. However, the EAT also held that he had not been carrying out his activities "at the appropriate time" which was at the time which accorded with the time off agreement at his workplace.

Transferring a representative to a **less satisfying job** or to a job where there was less opportunity to **earn bonuses or tips** could also come within the definition of action short of dismissal.

One issue which comes up more frequently is that of **annual appraisals** since employers may not be able to assess the performance of employees who spend a considerable amount of time on union activities under a workplace agreement. This becomes a particularly important issue where appraisal is used to determine pay. In some workplaces the solution has been for representatives to be awarded the average appraisal of the groups which they represent.

Without an agreement on how appraisals are to be dealt with difficulties can arise. In the case of *Thomas v The Post Office* (a 1981 unreported case) the tribunal agreed that a manager's inability to complete a performance appraisal for the representative did amount to "action short of dismissal" but found on the facts that its aim was not to deter him from carrying out his union activities.

Not every action taken by an employer will come within the definition of action to deter union activity. In one case (*Grogan v BRB, unreported 1978*) the employer took down some union notices on the grounds that they were "inflammatory" and warned the representative that disciplinary action would be taken against him if he did this again. The EAT said this didn't come within *section 146*.

Promotion

One of the concerns which union representatives express is that their union activities will influence management when it comes to their seeking promotion and that employers might use the rep's activities as a reason not to promote. Any employer doing this is breaking the law. In one case an employee who had recently become a union representative was told that she had a "less than encouraging attitude".

When she applied for promotion she was asked at interview whether she could foresee a conflict of interest between her job and the union. None of the other candidates for the post were asked this question. The industrial tribunal found that the employer had contravened *section 146*.

The case of *Wake v British Aerospace (unreported 1978)* involved a failure to promote. The facts were as follows:

> Mr Wake was a workplace representative. Although the company usually promoted on seniority it failed to select him as the most senior of the candidates for three posts.

There the employers successfully argued that the reason why he had not been selected was unrelated to his union activities but was based on his "immaturity" which made him unsuitable for the job.

More recently, in the case of *Gallagher v Dept of Transport [1994] IRLR 231*, this narrow view was upheld. Gallagher applied for a promoted post and was rejected. The reason given was that he had not been able to develop managerial skills due to the length of time he had spent on his union duties. He was advised to reduce or terminate his union activities if he wanted to acquire the experience.

Gallagher claimed that this action fell within the *section 146* definition. The Court of Appeal, to which the case was eventually referred, ruled that he could not pursue a *section 146* claim. The employer's purpose in not promoting him was to do with their wish that only those with the relevant experience be promoted and not to do with preventing him from carrying out his union duties.

Dismissal

Section 152 TULR(C)A 1992 makes it unlawful to dismiss an individual on the grounds of their union activities except where these activities involve industrial action. In addition *paragraph 15(b)* of the *ACAS Code on disciplinary practice and procedures in employment* says that because "disciplinary action against a trade union official can lead to a serious dispute" no disciplinary action beyond a formal warning should be taken without the case having been discussed first with a senior union representative or full time official. This means that before a trade union representative is dismissed the union at senior level should be contacted.

Paragraph 15b is not limited to cases where the dismissal is allegedly for trade union reasons. In the case of *Regan v LB Newham (unreported 1980)* the employee was dismissed for his "uncooperative" attitude. Shortly before his dismissal he was elected as branch chair of the union. The initial tribunal ruled against him on the grounds that he had **not been dismissed because of his union activities** and that paragraph 15(b) was therefore not relevant. The EAT reversed this decision pointing out that the code should be taken account of whenever disciplinary action was anticipated against a union representative.

It is for the employer to show the reason for dismissal and to prove that it comes within the category of "fair" dismissals permissable under law. This point was established some years ago in the case of *Maund v Penwith DC [1984] IRLR 24*. The facts were as follows:

> Alec Maund was a council worker in the architect's department but was also the chair of the union. He was dismissed for redundancy following a reorganisation which privatised the work he was doing. Maund claimed that the employers had been motivated by a desire to get rid of him because of his union position.

At the Court of Appeal his claim that it was up to the employers to explain why he was dismissed, was upheld. Lord Justice Griffiths said that "the legal burden of proving the reason for the dismissal is, by the wording of the Act, placed on the shoulders of the employer". If the employee alleges that there is another reason for the dismissal then the burden of proof shifts to the employee. But, according to Griffiths "this burden is a lighter burden", and it is enough for the employee to produce some evidence to raise doubt about the professed reason for dismissal for the burden of proof then to shift back to the employee.

The one specific risk which a representative faces is being singled out for dismissal in cases of **unofficial industrial action**. Under *section 237* of the 1992 Act an employee cannot complain of unfair dismissal if "at the time of dismissal he was taking part in an unofficial strike or other unofficial industrial action". Although an employer cannot lawfully victimise individuals taking official action (employers can only dismiss all strikers or none) they can select in unofficial disputes. If they are going to do so then it is likely that the target will be the union activist(s), invariably the workplace representative.

Redundancy selection

Trade unionists have the right to have cases of discrimination against them dealt with under the same principles as apply in other areas of discrimination law according to the EAT in the case of *Dundon v GPT [1995] IRLR 403*. Dundon's case is important because it established that selecting someone for redundancy on the basis that they had spent too much time on union business is **automatically unfair** even if the employer was not motivated by malice.

David Dundon was the senior rep at GPT. As such he spent a considerable amount of his day on union business. Although his employers told him to reduce his union time off, in practice they took no action to change his routine. However, when redundancies were announced and work absence was chosen as one of the criteria for selection Dundon found himself chosen.

The EAT noted that his selection was directly related to his union activities and that once the employer had granted time off and not taken reasonable steps to set its limits, any redundancy selection on that basis was a selection for trade union reasons and automatically unfair.

The case of *Driver v Cleveland Structural Engineering [1994] IRLR 636* is also relevant in showing how the law operates. The facts were as follows:

> Mr Driver was a steel erector. He had been working for less than two years when selected for redundancy. During his period in work he had acted as shop steward for the engineering union's members. Others with less service than him were offered alternative work.

Driver could not claim under the normal rules for unfair dismissal because he had worked less than two years. However, he could succeed if he was able to claim dismissal on trade union grounds since this, as automatically unfair grounds, requires no minimum service. Mr Justice Mummery in the EAT upheld his appeal. Although he accepted that the employer had no legal obligation to offer alternative employment to Driver, the fact that they did not was relevant in deciding on the issue of whether or not the real reason for dismissal was his trade union activities.

However, representatives also need to be aware of the risks of redundancy selection where they **transfer** to work to enable them to carry out union duties better. In the recent case of *O'Dea v ISC Chemicals [1995]* the Court of Appeal ruled that selection for redundancy of the union representative was fair when the job he was allocated to do was made redundant, even though his substantive job was not.

Applying for interim relief

If you are dismissed and believe that this was on the grounds of your trade union activities you can make an application for what is called "interim relief". This procedure, is available under *section 161 TULR(C)A 1992*. Using the procedure a trade union member can ask the tribunal to give a prompt hearing to the initial claim that the dismissal is on the grounds of trade union activities. If, in the view of the tribunal, there is a pretty good chance that a *section 152* dismissal has occurred, then the tribunal can order the employer to reinstate or re-engage the employee pending a full hearing on the complaint.

To use *section 161* procedure you must present a certificate in writing, signed by an authorised official of your union, which states that on the date of dismissal you were a union member and your membership or activities appear to be the grounds for your dismissal.

This certificate has to be presented **within seven days** of the date of dismissal. And, for the purposes of *section 161,* the date of dismissal is taken to be the **date on which dismissal notice** was given or, if there was no notice, the effective date of termination.

The case of *Sulemany v Habib Bank [1983] ICR 60* shows how the procedures operate. The facts were as follows:

> Mr Sulemany was a workplace representative for the bank union BIFU. He presented a certificate claiming interim relief but this initially was rejected because the industrial tribunal viewed it as inadequate. It did not state that he was a BIFU member nor that he had reasonable grounds for believing that he had been dismissed for union reasons.

The EAT reversed the tribunal ruling on the grounds that it was too technical in its interpretation of the *section 161* provisions. Reading the certificate in conjunction with Sulemany's application, in the IT1 form to the tribunal, it was obvious what the basis of his claim was. However, it should be noted that although he won on these points, the EAT ruled that the officer signing the form was not an "authorised union official" and that, on these grounds the application was invalid. In so ruling the EAT was following an earlier 1976 ruling (*Farmeary v Veterinary Drug Co [1976] IRLR 322*) that said there must be specific proof of authorization because it did not follow that all union officials fitted the description of "authorised" officials.

An application for interim relief will not be rejected because the certificate does not refer to *section 161 (Barley v Amey Roadstone Corp [1977] ICR 546).*

Conclusion

This booklet has set out to explain how the law affects you as a representative. Knowing about the law, both the rights it offers and the risks it presents, is vital for every representative who wants to make a real difference to conditions at work, not just for themselves but for every member they represent.

At the end of the day the most important element in being a good representative is in having the backing of all the workforce. Workers who have confidence in their representatives are much more likely to give them that backing and that confidence comes from knowing that the rep is capable of doing the job. This booklet will have served its purpose if representatives, armed with the information it provides, feel able to do their job better.

BARGAINING report

the only monthly negotiators'
guide written from a
trade union point of view

Bargaining Report is a recognised and leading source of information on all areas of collective bargaining at work, providing the facts shop stewards and reps need for effective negotiating.

Each issue contains the latest key negotiating statistics drawn from the Labour Research Department pay and conditions database of over 1,500 collective agreements.

It also covers new developments and guidelines relating to health and safety and the law at work.

Workplace issues of current concern to reps are examined in detail in our monthly surveys and features.

For information about subscription rates and a free sample copy of our latest issue, please fill in the box below and return to the Labour Research Department, 78 Blackfriars Road, London SE1 8HF.

Please send me information about subscribing to Bargaining Report and a free sample of the latest issue.

Name ....

Union ....

Address ....

.... Postcode ....